Play

with a purpose

with weather and animals

BrambleKids

INTRODUCTION

The need for a 'go-to' activity is essential for every busy parent and teacher!

These activities are enjoyable and engaging. They afford valuable learning and development opportunities for children, from physical and intellectual to emotional and social skills. They require only the use of everyday objects, making them perfect for the home or classroom.

Children can work on these fun tasks either independently, with their peers or with adult help.

New from Old

The educational crafts in this book will also teach children about RECYCLING. Many of the materials needed can be found around the home and then turned into something exciting by the children.

Curriculum Links

With a focus on weather and animals, these theme-based activities will improve children's understanding of familiar ideas and objects. Topics such as rainfall, clouds, wind and snowflakes form part of early teaching, as of course, does learning about animal life. These activities will inspire children's curiosity and fascination about the world, understanding its physical processes and the formation of environments. This understanding is an ideal preparation and support for school-based learning.

CONTENTS

WEATHER PROJECTS

1. You will need — 6-7
2. Keep a Sunshine Chart — 8-9
3. Make a Windmill — 10-11
4. Make a Weather Chart — 12-13
5. Make a Wind Chart — 14
6. Make Frost Patterns — 15
7. Make a Cloud Chart — 16-17
8. Make a Snowflake Pattern — 18
9. Make more Snowflakes — 19
10. Make a Weather Folder — 20
11. Make Rainbow Colours … or not — 21

Take Care!

Some of the activities in this book will require adult supervision. Encourage children to use scissors and pointed utensils with care and in a safe manner, further helping to build their skills and confidence.

ANIMAL PROJECTS

12. Make a Paper Butterfly — 22-23
13. Make a String-Holder Cat — 24-25
14. Make a Frog Bean Bag — 26
15. Make Egg Box Animals — 27
16. Make a Hedgehog — 28
17. Make Butterfly Blots — 29
18. Make a Crocodile — 30-31
19. Make a Woolly Dormouse — 32-33
20. Make Animal Silhouettes — 34
21. Make a Cotton Reel Snake — 35
22. Make a Cone Mouse — 35
23. Make a Milk Carton Menagerie — 36
24. Make an Aquarium — 38-39
25. Make a Hairy Caterpillar — 40-41
26. Make a Draught-Stopper Snake — 42
27. Make a Felt Snail — 43
28. Make a Horse — 44-45
29. Make a Wriggling Caterpillar — 46
30. Make some Pet Stones — 47

Development Links

Physical Skills

* Development of fine motor skills
  All these activities require the movement of hands and fingers. These in turn will involve the use and practice of fine motor skills and the general improvement of muscle control and strength. Developing these skills will extend into everyday activities such as washing and dressing.

* Increase in dexterity
  All these activities require manual dexterity. With practice and time, finer artistic skills will increase.

* Improvements in hand-eye coordination
  These activities require keen hand-eye coordination and such practice will support the development in further areas such as sports.

Intellectual Skills

* Promotion of innovation and creativity
  These activities offer children opportunities to create something new. This will encourage them to think differently and to innovate ideas.

* Development of problem-solving skills
  These activities require children to follow instructions and be resourceful. Encouraging them to work out where they may have gone wrong through discussion will support them in later life.

* Enhancement of decision-making skills
  Solving artistic challenges will promote correct and effective decision-making abilities. This will improve their ability to face other problems.

* Improvement in memory
  These activities require children to use and develop their visualising skills. Visualising complex designs will help improve memory.

* Improvements in visual processing
  These activities require children to identify patterns and colours that will naturally develop visual processing skills. This cognitive development is very important in early years.

Emotional and Social Skills

✳ Improvements in self-esteem
Encouraging children in these activities will boost their self-esteem. With each completed activity, children will feel a sense of achievement. Creating something allows children to feel in control and confident in themselves.

✳ Confident expression of self
Artistic activities encourage children to express themselves and your praise and encouragement will give them the confidence to do so. Children can channel negative and positive energy into these activities.

✳ Encouragement of creativity
Although instructed, all of the activities allow children to use their imagination and turn it into something productive. This will nurture artistic talents and self-esteem.

✳ Improvements in working with others
Encouraging children to work on these activities with their peers, whether they create a project together or simply support one another, will hugely develop their social skills and abilities. Interacting with other children with the same interests, or working together to overcome differences, will allow for friendships to develop.

✳ Strengthening of bonds
Working together with the child on these activities as a parent or teacher will strengthen your bond. Company will promote the children's enjoyment and engagement with the activity.

1 You will need

This book uses things that are usually found around the house or even things that might normally get thrown away. There are just a few things that might need to be purchased especially.

scissors

ruler

paints

sticky tape

string

paintbrushes

cardboard or kitchen roll

balls of wool

needle and thread

toothpicks or cocktail sticks

TIP

A note about glue

There are three types of glue we have used: school glue or paste, PVA and glue sticks. If you are sticking paper and card together, then a glue stick is the best one to use. School glue is best for papier mâché and PVA is best for heavier things, hard surfaces and wool. You can also use PVA as a kind of varnish. If you paint it onto a surface, it will go shiny when it dries.

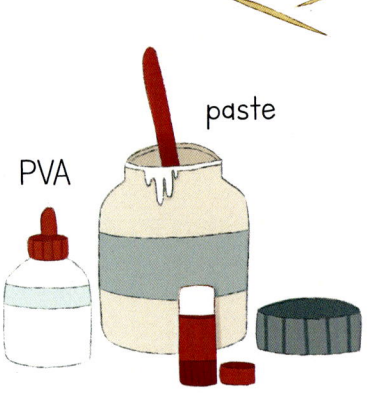

paste

PVA

glue stick

How to Make Papier Mâché

Papier mâché is a really fun material to make. It's a mix of paper and glue, or flour and water paste, which hardens when it dries. You can build up layers of paper to mould a vase or a bowl, or scrunch up torn newspaper pieces to make the shape of an animal or person.

Papier mâché takes a long time to dry, so wait before you paint or decorate it.

Things to Remember

If you are covering an object to make a papier-mâché mould, it's best to cover the object in cling film to start with. Use school glue or flour mixed with water into a thick paste. The more layers you add, the firmer your shape will be. Make sure the paper is really soggy with paste for the best results. It won't be waterproof.

sticks or twigs

vegetable oil

buttons

coloured paper

seeds and rice

bowl and old spoon

pine cones

pegs

compass

2 Keep a Sunshine Chart

Make a sunshine chart to record the number of sunny days during the next four weeks.

You will need

A large piece of card
Yellow paper
Scissors
Coloured felt-tip pens
Glue
A very large round plate

1 Draw around the plate onto the piece of card. Cut out the circle you just drew.

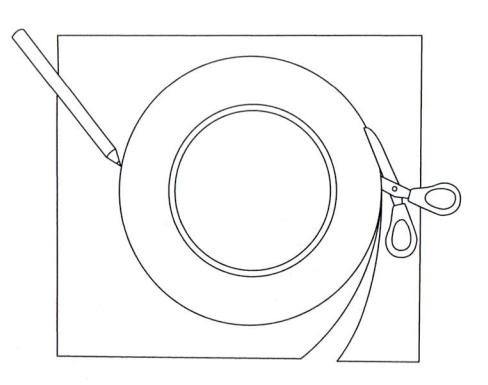

2 Fold the circle in half. Fold it in half again.

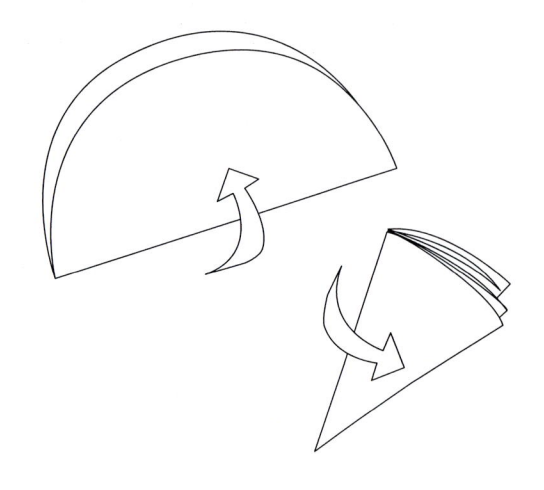

3 Open up the card. Draw seven lines at equal distances from each other from the centre of the circle to the outside edge of the four sections. You will have 28 lines and a space for each day.

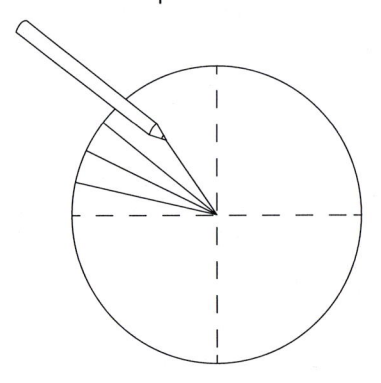

4 Snip the leftover card scraps into points for the sun's rays. Decorate the chart with the sun's rays, and mount it on the wall.

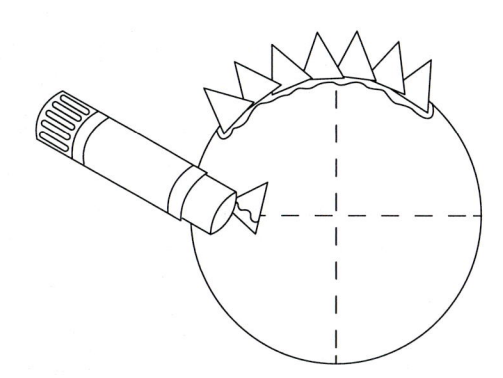

5 Cut out the paper shapes to show sunshine, patches of sunshine and no sunshine. Glue the correct shape to each day.

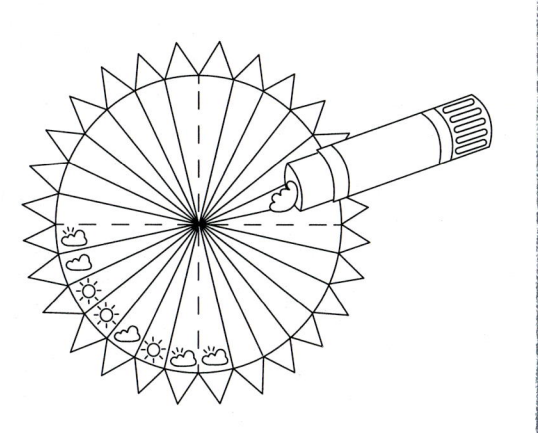

3 Make a windmill

You will need

Square paper

Coloured paints or crayons

A paper fastener

A paper straw

1 Fold the square, corner to corner, then unfold. Colour each triangle brightly on both sides of the paper.

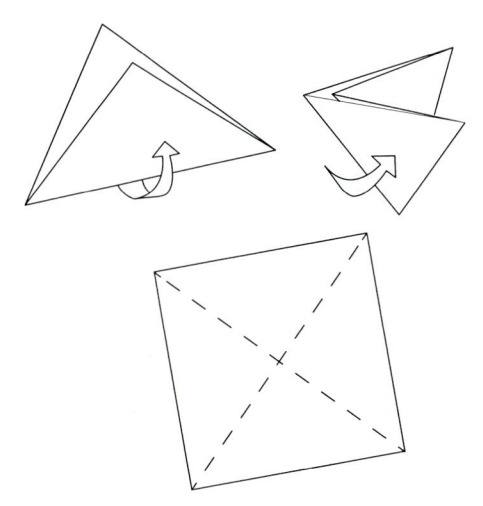

2 Make a pencil mark about two centimetres (cm) from the centre on all four fold lines. Cut along each fold and stop at the pencil marks.

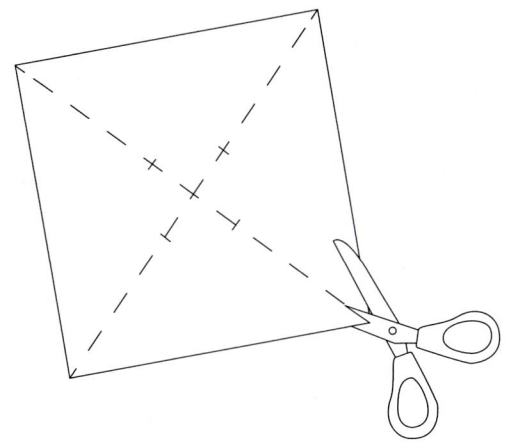

3 Bring every other point into the centre and hold the points down. Make a small hole in the centre of the back and poke a paper fastener through them all to fix them in place.

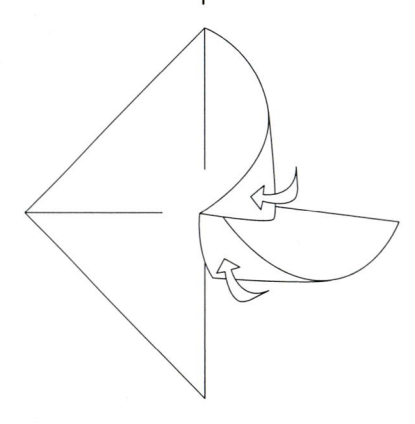

4 Then make a small hole through one end of the straw and push the paper fastener through that too. Then you will have a finished windmill.

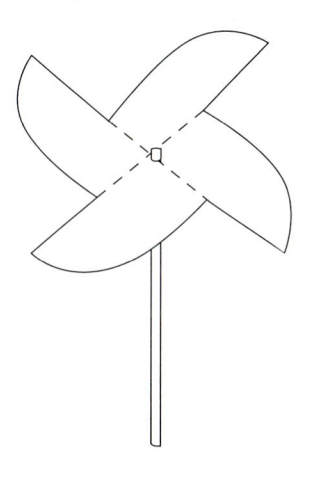

TIP Make sure that the windmill turns easily on the paper fastener without catching. If it does, you will find that it will spin around just as easily if you hold it up to the wind.

4 Make a weather chart

Watch the sky each evening for a week and make a weather chart to record your findings.

You will need

A sheet of white paper or card
Coloured crayons
A pencil and ruler

1 Draw the lines across and down to make a chart like this.

	Sunday	Monday	Tuesday	Wednesday	Thursday	Friday	Saturday
Morning							
Afternoon							

2 Each evening draw symbols like these to record the day's weather. Try to find out the wind speed and the day's temperature too.

Cloudy   Windy   Sunny   Rain   Foggy   Snow

12

13

5 Make a Wind Chart

Keep a record of the direction in which the wind blows each day.

You will need

A large sheet of white card
Pencil
Compass
Handkerchief

1 If you want to record a week, make a chart like this with spaces to record the wind for seven days. Mark on the points of the compass as shown. Colour the centre in black.

2 Use your compass on the first day to show you which direction is north, and turn your chart north in the same direction. Then hold up a handkerchief or watch the direction that the trees are swaying to decide where the wind is blowing from.

3 Each day colour in a square on the appropriate arm of your chart to mark the direction of the wind. Working towards the centre, colour in the outer square on the first day, the next one in on the second day, and so on.

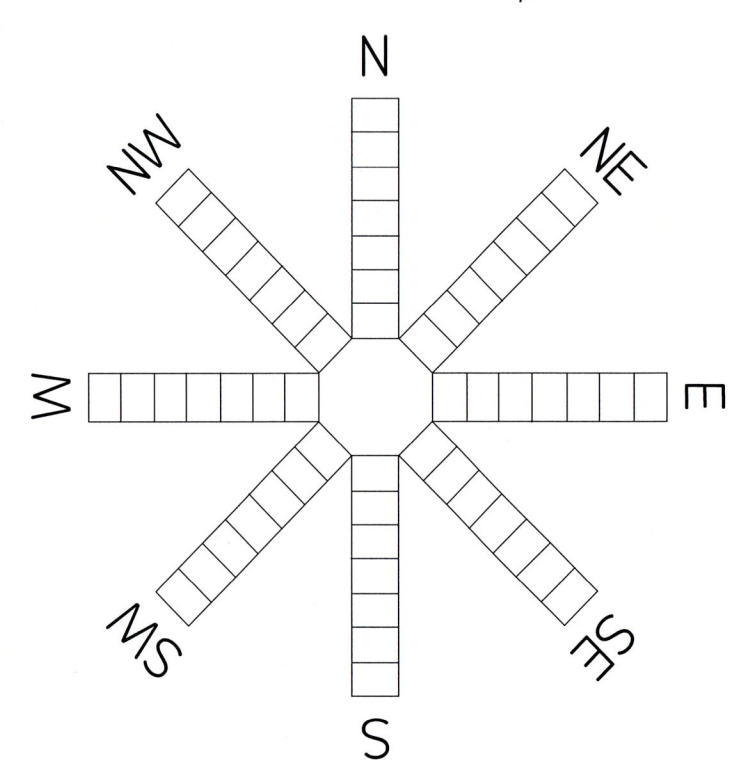

6 Make Frost Patterns

You will need

White poster paint
A brush
Thin paste
Sheet of dark-coloured card

1 Mix a little paste with the white paint and stir well. Brush this mixture quite thickly over the coloured card.

2 With your nails or fingertips, make patterns in the white paste. Keep your fingers tightly together and turn and twist them. Make loops and swirls and fern-like shapes.

7 Make a cloud chart

Keep a daily record of the clouds you see in the sky by drawing them as symbols on a chart.

You will need
A sheet of white paper or card
Coloured crayons
A pencil and ruler

1 Using your pencil and ruler, draw lines down and across to make a chart for a month.

2 Have a look at the different cloud shapes you might see on the opposite page. Draw them as simple symbols.

3 Whenever you see a cloud, draw its symbol on the chart in the box for that day.

16

Cloud Shapes

White, fluffy cotton-wool clouds seen on sunny days. These sometimes bring showers.

A grey sheet of cloud covering the sky on dull, windless days. They often mean drizzle.

Thin wispy clouds high in the sky on a fine day.

High piles of grey clouds usually mean rain and wind.

Heavy black and grey clouds often bring heavy rain and sometimes thunderstorms.

8 Make a Snowflake Pattern

If you looked at a snowflake under a microscope you would see a beautiful pattern. It is very delicate and light. Can you make one from paper? It would be a good way of decorating your weather charts.

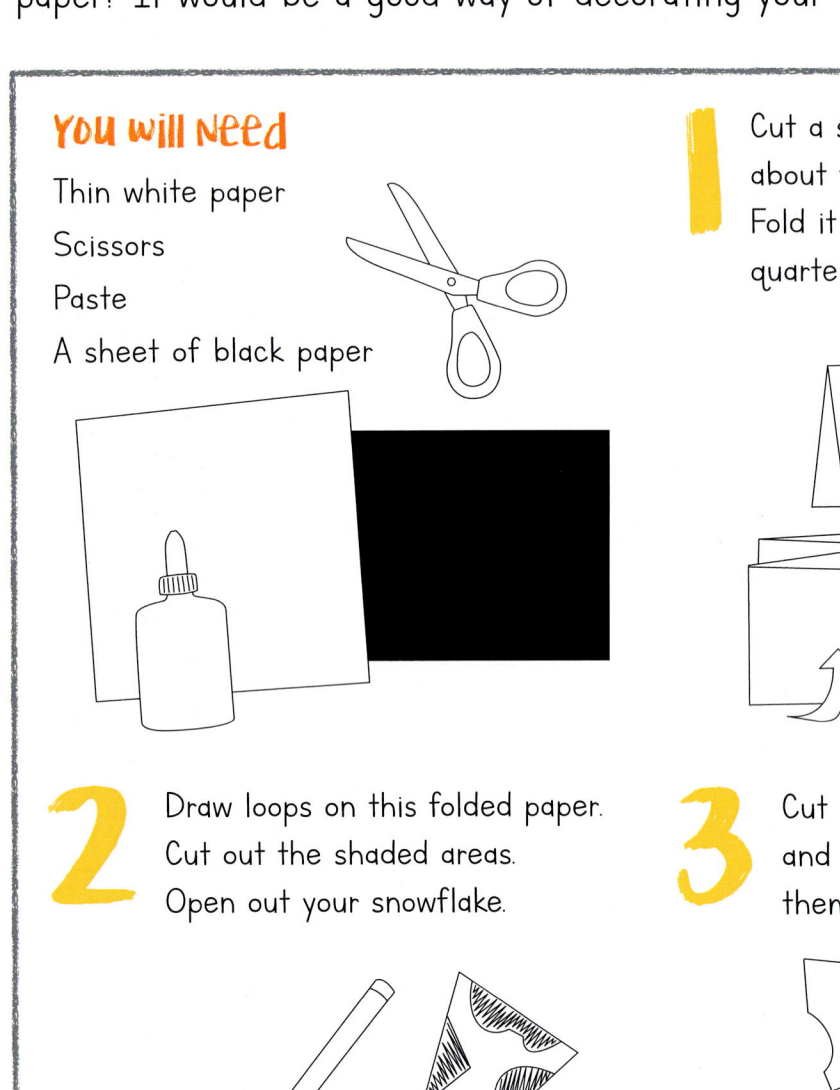

You will need
Thin white paper
Scissors
Paste
A sheet of black paper

1 Cut a square of white paper about the size of a handkerchief. Fold it in half and then into quarters. Fold once again.

2 Draw loops on this folded paper. Cut out the shaded areas. Open out your snowflake.

3 Cut more, making them smaller and smaller, and then stick them onto the black paper.

9 Make More Snowflakes

You will need

White paper
Pencil
Scissors
Yoghurt pot

1 On your paper draw a circle around the yoghurt pot and cut it out. Fold the circle in half, then in quarters and eighths.

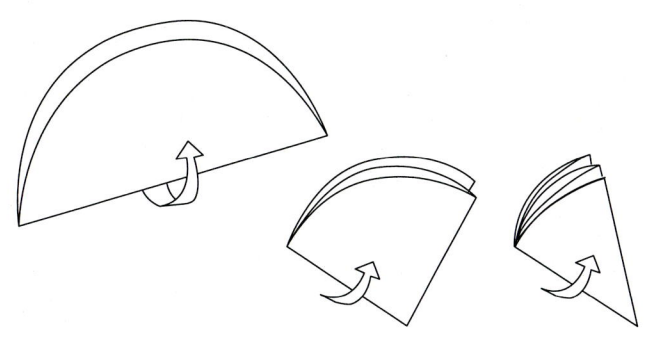

2 Shade in the area as shown. Cut out this shaded area.

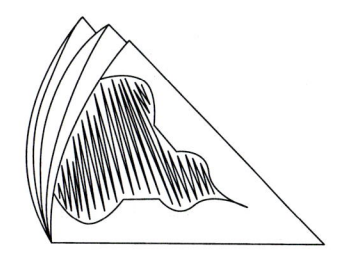

3 Open up your snowflake and stick either onto black paper or onto the window during winter for the best effect.

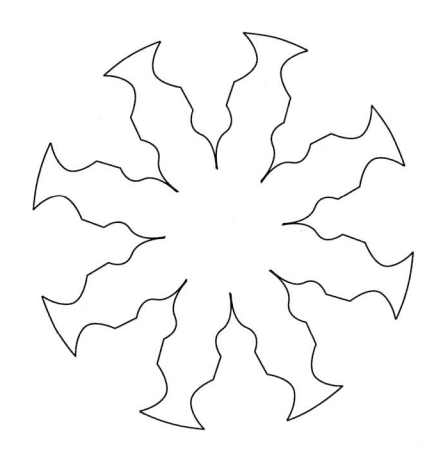

19

10 Make a weather folder

Why not make a folder out of thin card to hold all your weather information?

You will need

A large sheet of paper or card
Coloured crayons, paint or pencils
Glue or sticky tape

1 Fold a large sheet of card in three as shown in the diagram and decorate the front with different kinds of weather symbols or snowflake patterns.

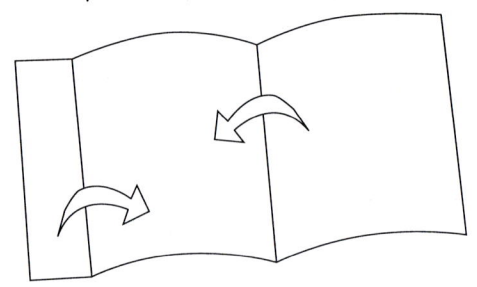

2 Print W E A T H E R neatly on the front. Make sure the folder is big enough to hold all your charts.

3 Glue the small fold to the back of the folder and tape the bottom to form a pocket where you can store all your information.

11 Rainbow Colours ... or Not

You will need

A circle of white cardboard about 10–15 cm in diameter

2 pieces of string about 1 metre long

7 crayons in the colours of the rainbow (red, orange, yellow, green, blue, indigo and violet)

A sharp pencil

1 Draw seven lines on the card circle so there are seven equal sections. Colour each section with a different colour crayon.

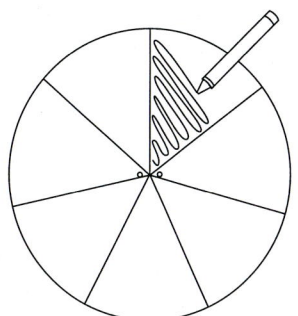

2 Carefully make two holes in the centre of the circle with the point of the pencil.

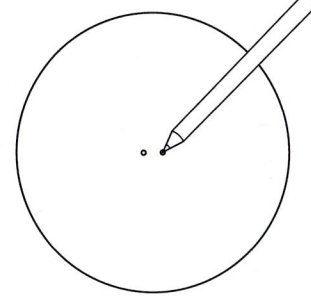

3 Thread one string through each hole and knot the strings together at each end.

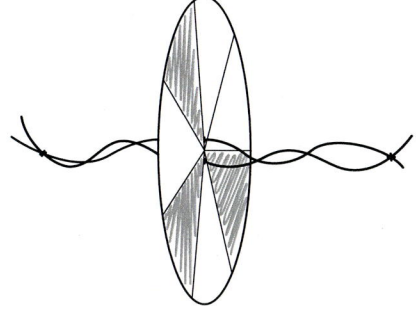

4 Twirl the card circle until the strings are tightly twisted.

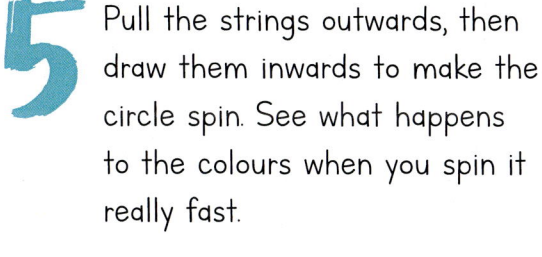

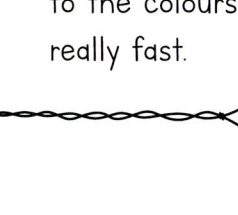

5 Pull the strings outwards, then draw them inwards to make the circle spin. See what happens to the colours when you spin it really fast.

12 Make a Paper Butterfly

Make sure that you use paper that is the same colour on both sides. It should not be white on the back.

You will need

2 sheets of different-coloured paper
A sheet of white paper
Scissors
Glue for paper
Pencil
PVA glue
Clothes peg

1 Place the two sheets of coloured paper together and draw a wing shape on the paper as shown here.

2 Cut through both sheets of paper along the pencil line.

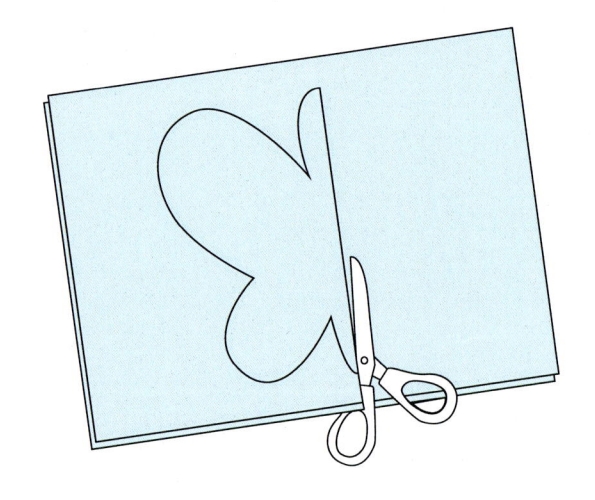

3 Lightly draw in the dotted lines on your cut out wings. Keeping the two wings firmly together, cut along the dotted lines.

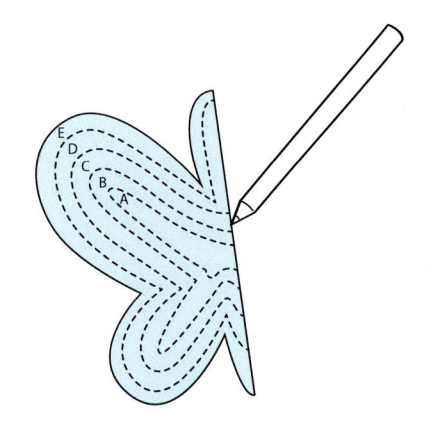

4 Place all your cut out pieces in front of you and stick onto the white paper in this order. Piece A in one colour opposite A in the other colour. Then follow with B to B, C to C, D to D, and E to E.

5 Cut out the butterfly and paste it on to the side edge of a clothes peg with PVA glue. Now you can clip your butterfly onto whatever you like.

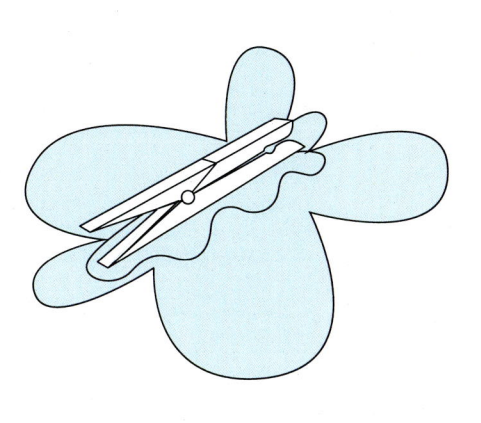

TIP You can also make this butterfly in felts, and decorate it with sequins and beads.

13 Make a string-holder cat

You will need

Felt or stiff fabric
A small plate or saucer
Scissors
PVA glue
Pencil
A small coin
Scraps of coloured fabric
A small length of ribbon
A needle and cotton thread
4 broom bristles
A ball of string

1 Place the saucer on the felt and draw round it. Cut out the circle, then cut out another one exactly the same size. Make a small hole in the first circle and a long slit in the second.

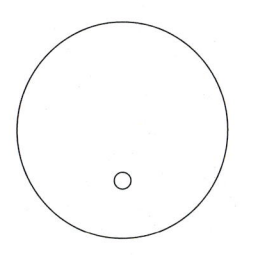

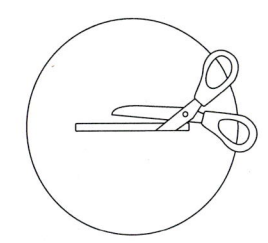

2 Using different fabrics, cut out the two eyes and a nose the size of a small coin and glue them onto the face.

3 Cut out two ears and glue them between the two circles. Fold a small piece of ribbon and glue it between the ears.

4 Now oversew the circles together neatly all the way round taking care to leave the ears and loop sticking up.

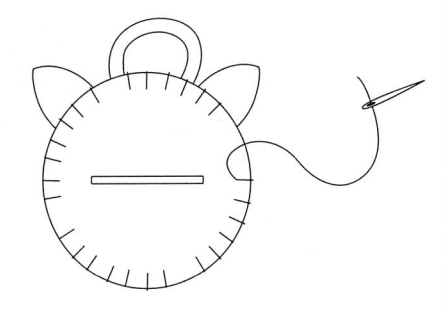

5 Push the four bristles through the material next to the nose to make the whiskers.

6 The ball of string goes through the slit at the back, and the end is pulled through the hole in the front.

14. Make a frog bean bag

You will need

Felt or other fabric in two colours
Scissors
Pins
PVA glue
A needle and cotton thread
Packet of dried rice or beans

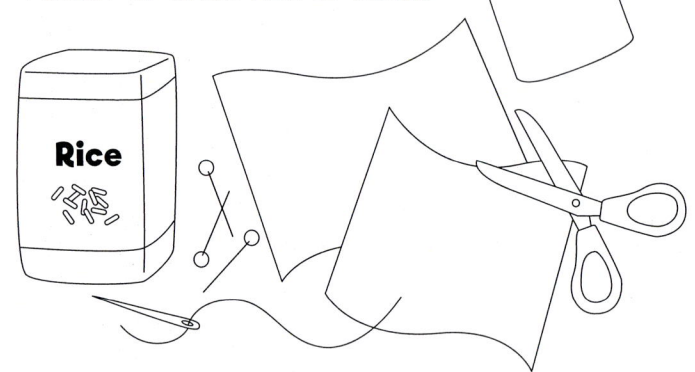

1 Fold the felt square in half and pin at the top. Draw a frog shape on your material. Cut this out and pin the shapes together leaving a small gap unpinned at the head.

2 Sew a running stitch around the frog, keeping about 1 cm from the edge. Leave a gap at the top. Turn inside out and fill with dried rice or beans.

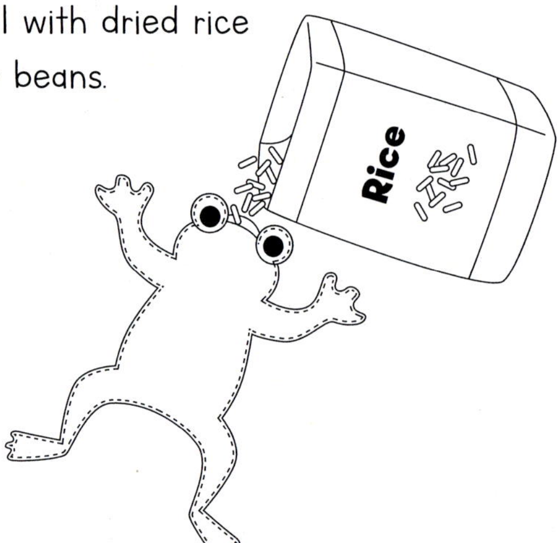

3 Turn the raw edges of the gap inside and oversew to close it. Cut out two large eyes and glue them on top of the head.

15 Make egg box animals

You will need

Some cardboard egg boxes
Scissors
A toilet roll tube
Glue or sticky tape
Paint
Paint brushes
String or wool

1 Cut the egg box into the individual cups. Use these cups or a toilet roll tube to make the body of the animal.

2 Cut shapes from the cups to make the heads, ears, legs, wings and so on.

3 Paint the animals and leave to dry.

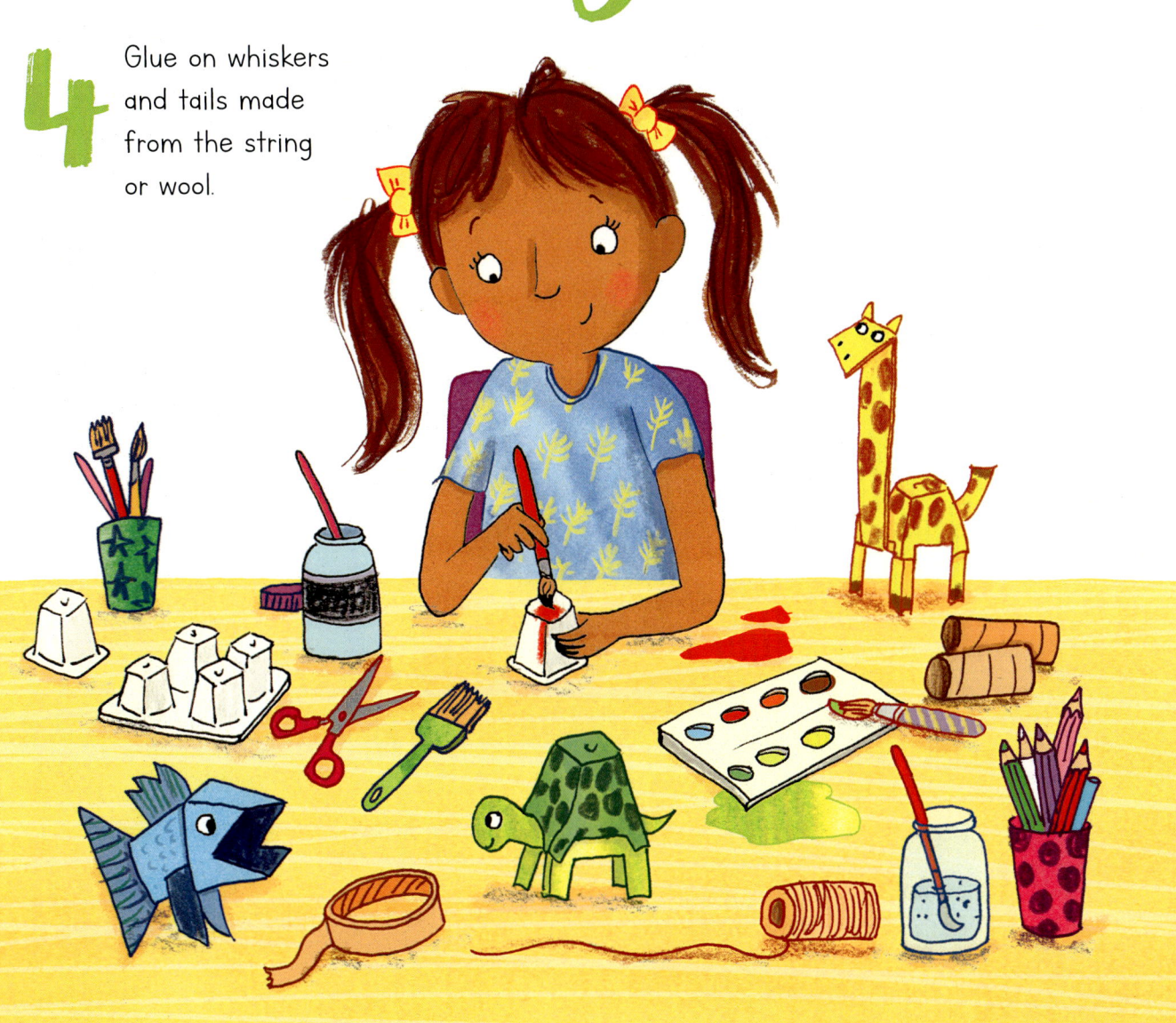

4 Glue on whiskers and tails made from the string or wool.

16 Make a hedgehog

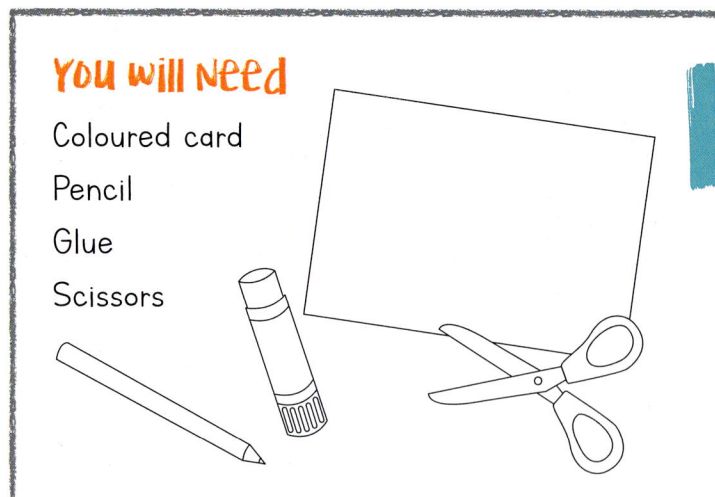

You will need
Coloured card
Pencil
Glue
Scissors

1 Cut a semi-circle of card. Fold it into three equal parts.

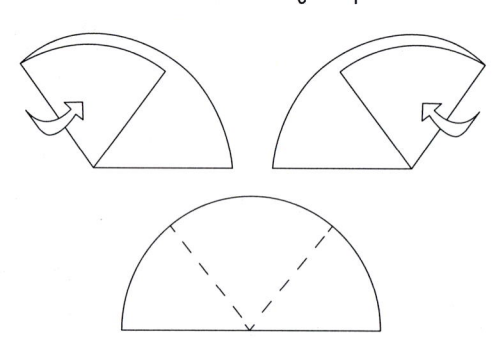

2 Cut six strips of paper long enough to reach from fold to fold across the hedgehog's back. Snip and curl each strip round a pencil.

3 Glue the curled strips of paper to the centre part of the card semi-circle so that they slightly overlap. Begin with the back layer and work towards the face.

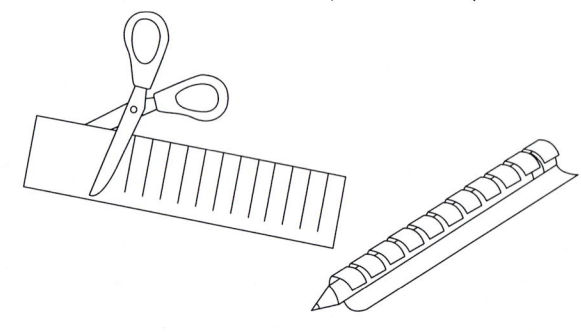

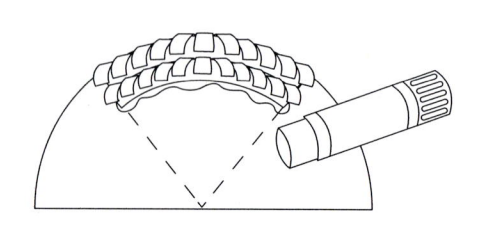

4 Fold on the dotted lines and glue or staple A across B.

5 Make this face in paper and glue it to the point of the folds.

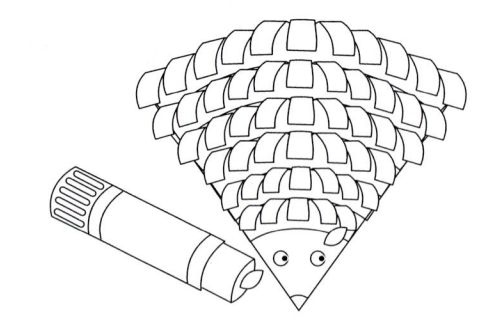

28

17 Make butterfly blots

You will need

A sheet of paper
Different-coloured paints
A spoon for each colour of paint

1 Fold the sheet of paper down the middle, then open it out flat.

2 Spoon blobs of paint on to one half of the paper only.

3 Fold the other half over and press down firmly.

4 Now open out the paper and you should have a colourful butterfly.

18 Make a Crocodile

You will need

Some round-shaped balloons
Vaseline or cooking oil
Pieces of newspaper
Thin paste or glue
Paints and a brush
String
Large-eyed needle

1 Blow up the balloons to different sizes and knot the ends.

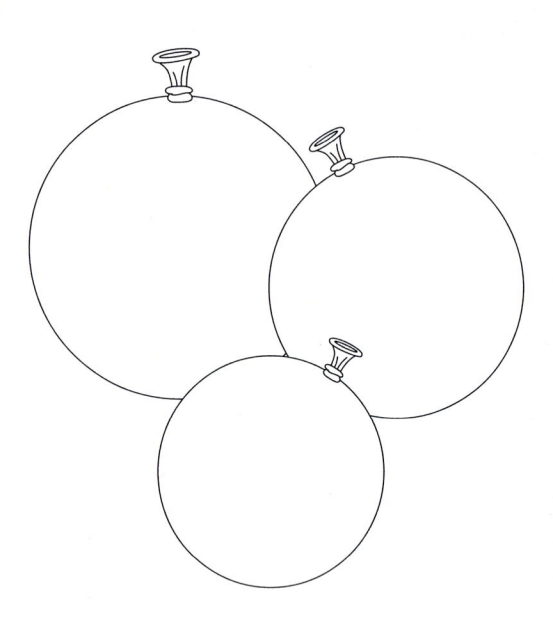

2 Smear the balloons with Vaseline or oil and cover with some layers of papier mâché made from the newspaper and paste, leaving the knot uncovered. Let them dry for 24 hours.

3 Pop the balloons with the needle and pull them carefully out of the dried papier-mâché shape.s. Flatten one of them a little to make the crocodile's head.

4 Paint the papier-mâché shapes and paint two eyes on the head. Leave to dry.

5 Thread the needle with strong cotton or wool and tie a knot in the end. Thread the smallest ball on, then the next smallest, and so on, until you get to the head. Tie another knot at the end.

19 Make a woolly dormouse

You will need

Cardboard
Yoghurt pot to draw around
A small coin
Scissors
Bits of felt
Odd balls of wool
Glue
Short lengths of thick string

1 Draw two circles on the cardboard using the bottom of the yoghurt pot. Cut them out. Then cut out a circle the size of a small coin in the middle of each one.

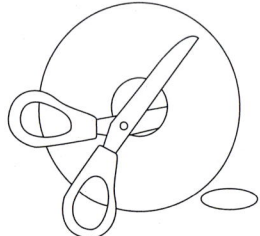

2 Put the two circles together and wind the wool round and round, joining on a different colour whenever you want to. Continue until it is really difficult to push the wool through the centre hole.

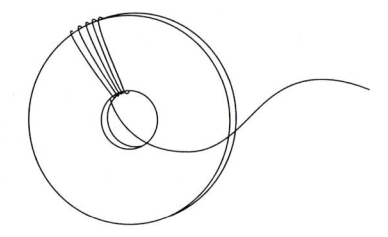

3 Cut the edge of the wool circles between the cardboard edges. Tie a piece of wool tightly between the cardboard circles, so that the wool is held firmly at the centre.

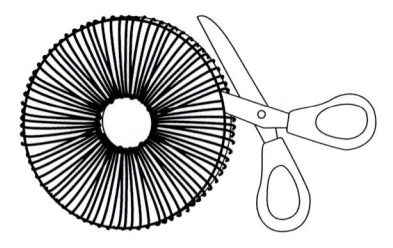

4 Cut away the cardboard circles and fluff out the wool. You may need to trim the ends a bit to make the pompom even.

5 Cut out small felt shapes for the eyes and ears and stick them onto the ball.

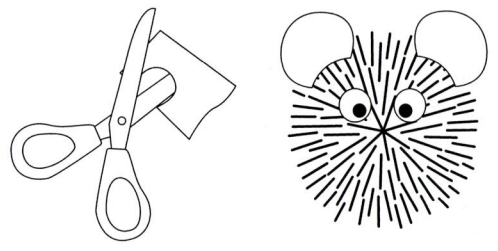

6 To make the tail, tie a length of thick string to the wool that holds the centre. Knot it near the end and fray the tips.

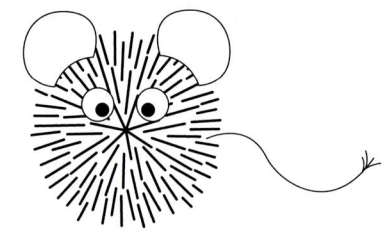

TIP Make two tiny pompoms for your cat to play with. Or make a really large dormouse, using saucer-sized circles, to sit on your bed.

20 Make animal silhouettes

You will need

Black paper
Chalk
Scissors
Large sheet of white paper
Paste and brush

1 Choose your favourite animals. Think of some you have seen in a zoo, or maybe a farm. Draw them on the black paper with chalk, then cut them out carefully and paste them onto the large white sheet.

2 Arrange them in a zoo or farmyard scene, drawing railings and trees and visitors around them.

21 Make a Cotton Reel Snake

You will need

As many used cotton reels as you can find
Thin string
A button
Coloured paints
Brushes

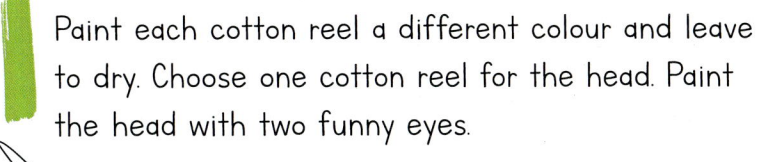

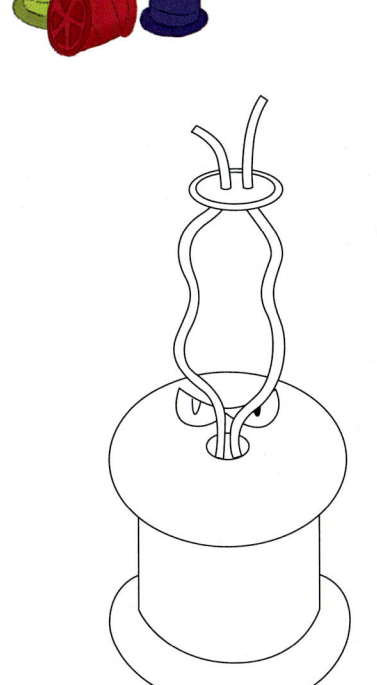

1 Paint each cotton reel a different colour and leave to dry. Choose one cotton reel for the head. Paint the head with two funny eyes.

2 Tie a large knot in the string, then thread it through all the reels. Leave 5 cm of string poking from the head and cut the string off.

3 Divide the string into two by untwisting it. Poke each end through a hole in the button. Knot twice and leave as the tongue.

22 Make a Cone Mouse

You will need
- A pine cone
- 2 small shells
- 2 large shells
- 4 bristles from a broom or stiff brush
- PVA glue
- Card

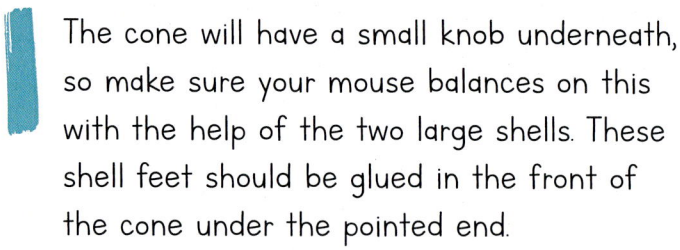

1 The cone will have a small knob underneath, so make sure your mouse balances on this with the help of the two large shells. These shell feet should be glued in the front of the cone under the pointed end.

2 The small shells can be glued either side of the pointed nose of the cone as eyes.

3 Cut two small triangles in the card for ears and glue them above the eyes.

4 If the flakes of the cone are slightly open at the nose end, stick the broom bristles firmly in to make whiskers.

23 Make a Milk Carton Menagerie

You will need

Some milk or juice cartons
A sheet of lightweight card
Scissors
Paper drinking straws
Some wool or string
Glue or sticky tape
Acrylic paint and paint brushes

1 Decide what animal you would like to make. This will tell you which way to stand the milk carton, either upright or on its side.

2 Cut out shapes from the card for ears, wings and paws, and glue these to your animal.

3 Paint and leave to dry.

4 Use the drinking straws and wool to make whiskers and tails. Then make some more!

TIP

Mix some washing-up liquid with the paint to help it stick to the cartons if you don't have acrylic paint.

37

24 Make an aquarium

You will need

A large cardboard box

Cellophane wrap

Coloured paper

Crayons or coloured pencils

Foil, glitter and sequins to decorate

String or cotton

Scissors

1 Cut large windows in all four sides of a cardboard box. Leave a firm border on each side as the frame of the tank. Make sure both the top and the bottom of the box are firm.

2 Glue sheets of blue or green cellophane wrap across the four sides of the aquarium to give a glistening watery effect.

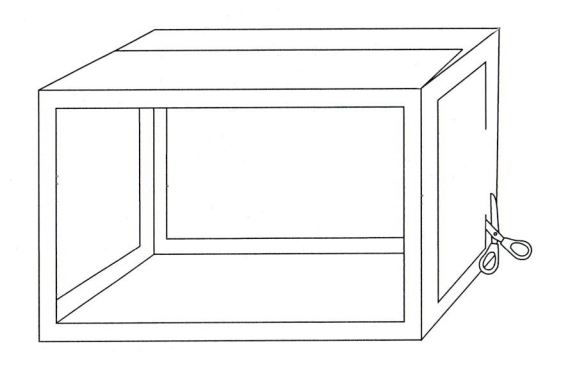

3 Cut out and decorate different shapes of fish, plants, shells and pebbles. Use gummed paper, shiny foils, glitter or sequins.

4 Thread the fish with cotton and hang them from the roof of the aquarium.

5 If you add a small tab to the other shapes, you can glue them to the bottom of the aquarium. Fold the tabs underneath to create a base that holds them upright...

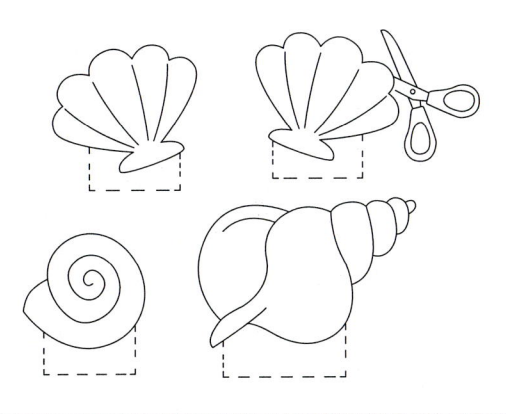

25 Make a hairy caterpillar

You will need
2 egg boxes
Strong glue
Paints
2 used matchsticks
A bean or round button
Wool or raffia
Coloured paper

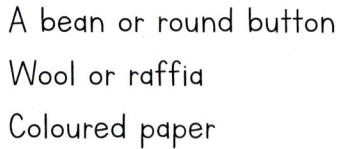

1 With strong glue, join the two egg boxes together by carefully overlapping the small rims. You can put the humps in different places by joining the ends in different ways. Make sure you have a suitable hump at the end for your caterpillar's head.

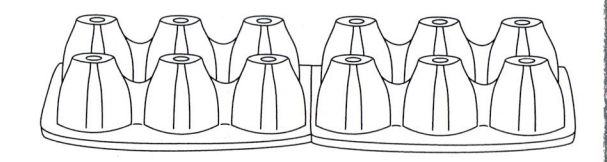

2 Paint the caterpillar very bright or very dark using mysterious colours, depending on the kind of caterpillar it is.

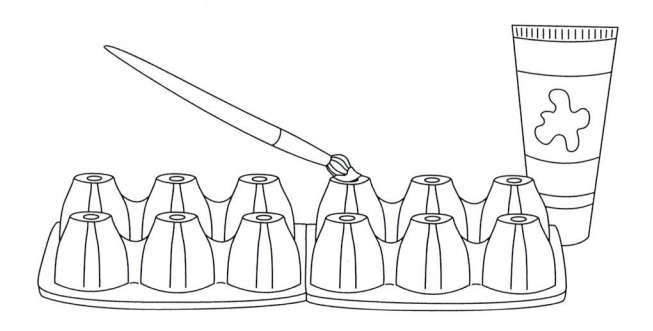

3 Stick two matchsticks through the head to make horns with eyes on the end of them.

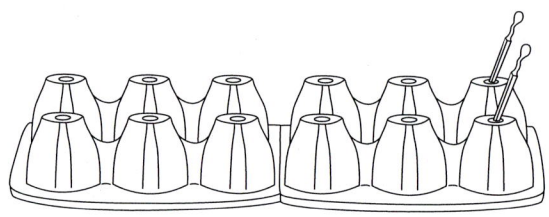

4 Cut short strands of wool or raffia and stick them over the head in shaggy tufts. Then cut a paper fringe and stick it all round the bottom of the body.

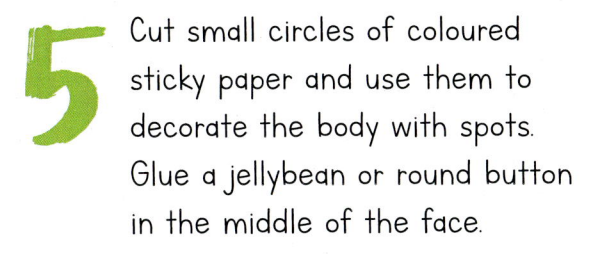

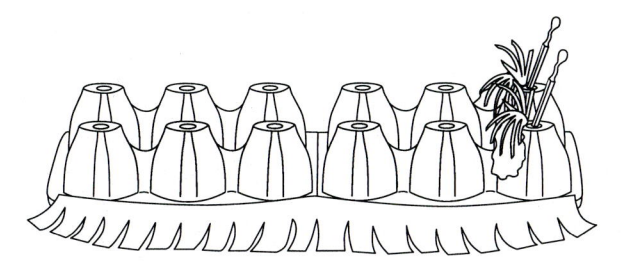

5 Cut small circles of coloured sticky paper and use them to decorate the body with spots. Glue a jellybean or round button in the middle of the face.

26 Make a draught-stopper snake

You will need

A length of hessian a little longer than the width of your door and about 45 cm wide

Needle

Thread

Scissors

Rags for stuffing

Scraps of material

Strong glue

2 buttons

1 Fold your material in half lengthwise and sew neatly along the edges until you are 15 cm from the end. Then sew the rest tapering inwards to the fold to make a rounded point

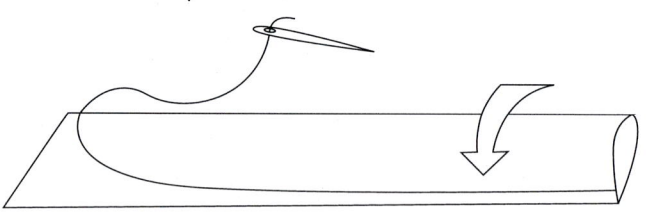

2 Turn the snake's body inside out and stuff it with rags. Sew the open end with running stitches, then gather it together and fasten off.

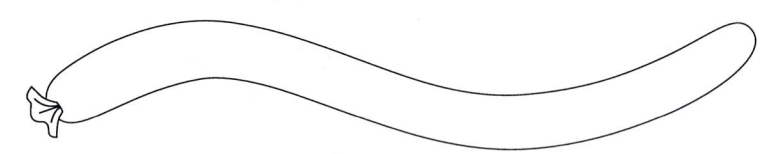

3 Cut strips of coloured material and glue them in bands around the body.

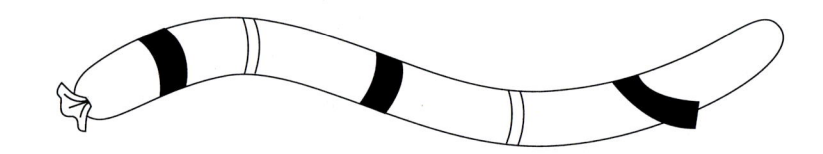

4 Cut a large circle and, pressing the gathered opening down flat, glue or sew the circle over the gathered hole so you cover the frayed edges. Sew two buttons above the circle for the snake's eyes.

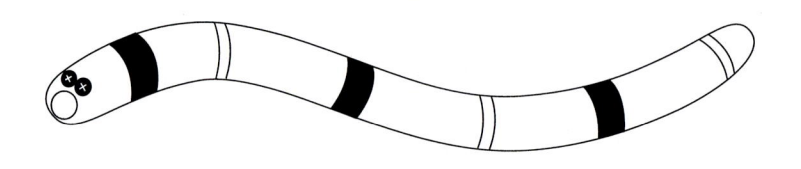

27 Make a Felt Snail

You will need

Felt square
Pencil
Cotton thread
Strong glue
Needle
Rags for stuffing
Buttons, corks, paper scraps, sequins
Scissors

1 Fold the felt square in half and pin at the top. Draw a snail shape using up as much of the felt as you can. Cut out two identical snail shapes with the scissors.

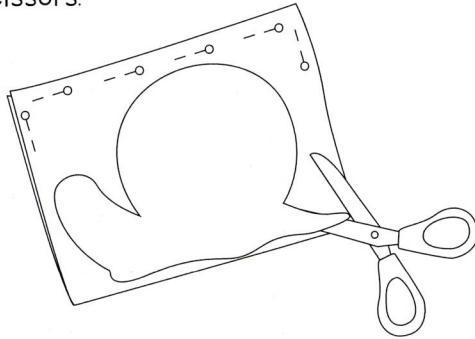

2 Decorate each side using coloured scraps and strong glue. With decorated sides facing out, stitch the two sides together leaving a small hole in the underside for the stuffing. Stuff with rags.

3 Stitch up the opening. You could put brush bristles through small beads or sequins to make the snail's horns.

28 Make a horse

You will need

A kitchen roll cardboard tube or a piece of card for the body
Coloured paper for the mane and tail
4 toilet roll tubes for the legs
Crayons or coloured pencils
Scissors
Glue for card

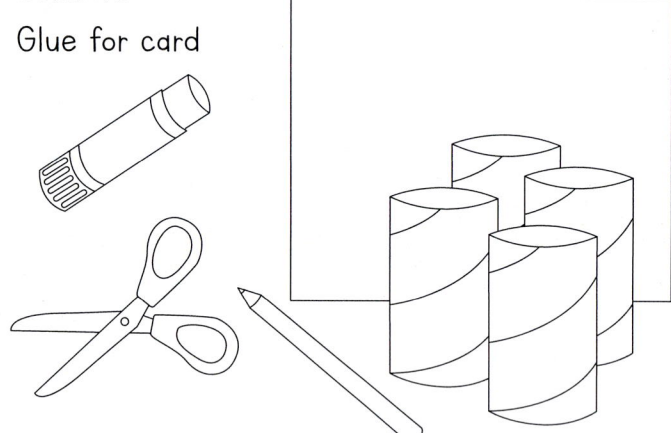

1 To make the body

Make a cylinder from card or use a cardboard tube from a kitchen roll, cut a smalls slit at the top. Then draw four circles underneath that are the exact size of the leg cylinders and cut them out.

2 To make the legs

Fold four toilet rolls or card so they will be able to push through the holes in the body cylinder.

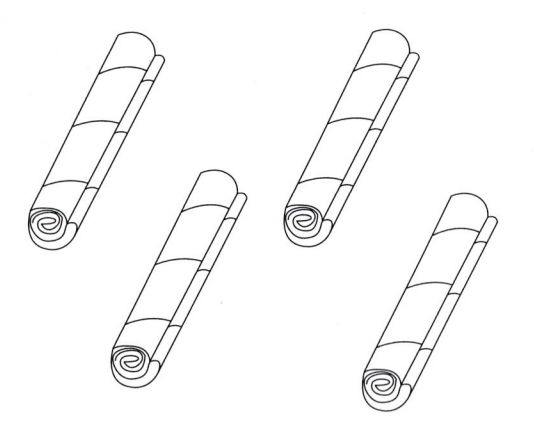

3 To make the mane

Cut a strip of paper for the mane. Snip one edge and curl it round a pencil.

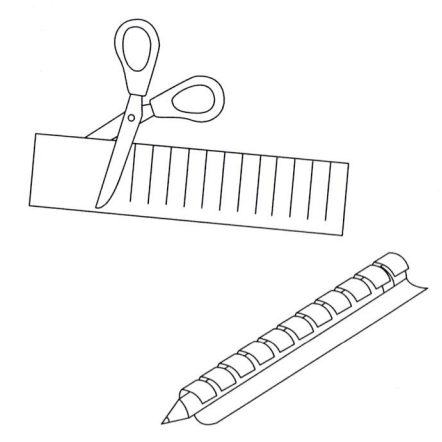

4 To make the head
Make the horse's head from stiff card. Attach the mane to it with glue. Then fit it in the slit in the top of the cylinder.

5 To make the tail
Make the tail from a piece of paper, snipped and curled. with a pencil. Glue to the back of the horse's body.

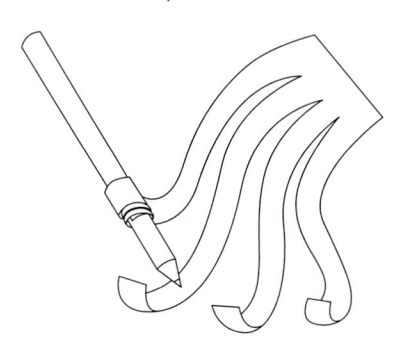

29 Make a wriggling caterpillar

You will need

A long piece of rod or a stick
Paper plates
Cotton thread
Strong glue
Needle
Buttons, corks, paper scraps, sequins
Scissors

1 Thread the top of each plate with cotton thread, using a large knot to anchor it at one end.

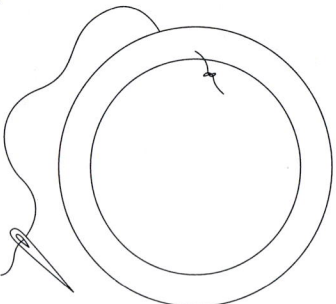

2 Decorate the first plate with a face of a caterpillar.

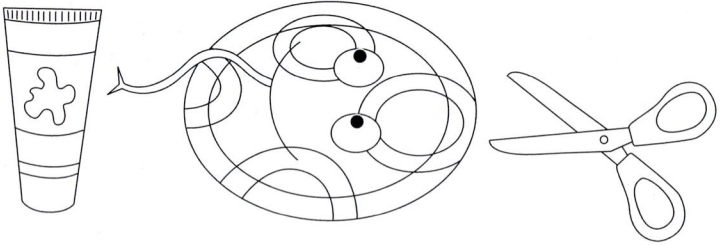

3 Decorate all the other plates for the body. Tie the cotton to the rod and hang. Now make your caterpillar wriggle.

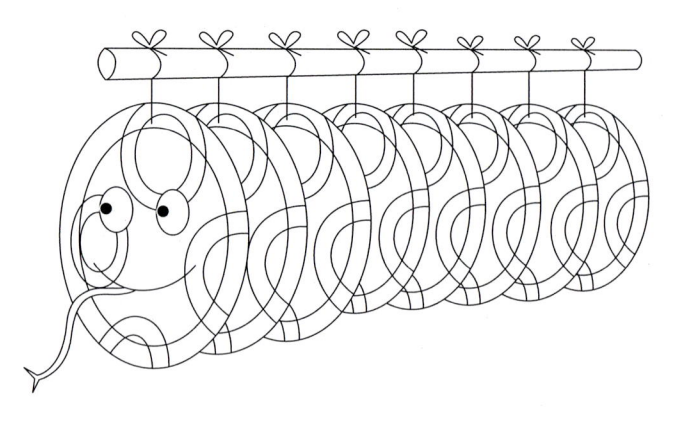

30 Make Some Pet Stones

You will need

A selection of smooth, clean, dry stones
Acrylic paints
Small paint brushes
Clear nail varnish

1 Look at each stone carefully to see if it reminds you of a particular animal. A flat, round stone might become a cat or frog. A short, oval-shaped stone might make a nice penguin.

2 Use coloured acrylic paints to paint your animal onto the stone.

3 When dry, use a clean brush to cover the stone with a thin layer of varnish.

WRITTEN BY: FELICIA LAW

EDUCATIONAL TEXT: AIMÉE JACKSON

DESIGN: SARAH PEDEN ASPINALL

COLOUR ILLUSTRATIONS: SARAH JENNINGS (THE BRIGHT AGENCY)

BLACK LINE ILLUSTRATIONS: KERI GREEN (BEEHIVE ILLUSTRATION AGENCY)

COPYRIGHT © 2021 BrambleKids Ltd

ISBN: 978-1-913189-56-3